"Adapting in the Age of AI: Millennials Can Stay Ahead ... Work"

Table of Contents:

Introduction: The Future is Already Here

Hey there, fellow Millennial. You're in a unique position. You've seen the world evolve — from dial-up internet to broadband, from flip phones to smartphones. You lived through the dot-com boom and bust, the Great Financial Crisis, COVID and now you're standing at the edge of another great transformation: the rise of artificial intelligence (AI).

You may already feel it. The buzz around automation, AI chatbots, self-driving cars, and machine learning is deafening. People are talking about the end of traditional jobs, the rise of robots, and whether AI will take over the world. But here's the thing: this isn't science fiction. This is all happening right now, in real time. And as an older Millennial, you're not too young to be affected, but you're not too old to adapt, either.

This book is for you. It's for those of us who grew up in a world that didn't have AI and now find ourselves navigating a landscape where it seems like everything is changing. It's easy to feel left behind. But with the right mindset, tools, and strategies, you can not only keep up with this change but thrive and profit in it. Let's explore how you can position yourself for success in a world where AI is a key player.

Chapter 1: The AI Revolution - Understanding What's Happening

Before diving into how to stay ahead, let's take a step back and look at what's actually going on. What is AI? How does it work? Why is it causing such a stir in almost every industry?

AI isn't just a buzzword. It refers to the ability of machines to learn from data, make decisions, and perform tasks that once required human intelligence. These tasks range from analyzing data and recommending products to writing emails and driving cars. It's a far-reaching technology that's already transforming industries from healthcare to finance to entertainment. It is as monumental as the Industrial Revolution.

Understanding the basics of AI — how it works, where it's headed, and its potential — is crucial for staying ahead. And you don't need a degree in computer science to do this. You just need a little curiosity and a willingness to learn.

The Age of AI: A Brief Overview

To understand how AI is transforming the world, it's essential to first grasp what AI actually is. Artificial intelligence (AI) refers to a broad category of technologies that aim to mimic human intelligence. AI isn't just about robots or futuristic sci-fi movies. It's already embedded in our lives in ways we don't even notice.

At its core, AI involves machines or software that can perform tasks that traditionally required human intelligence. These tasks include things like:

- **Problem-solving** (AI can process large amounts of data to identify patterns or solutions)

- **Speech recognition** (think about how Siri or Alexa understands your voice)

- **Decision-making** (AI systems are used in everything from recommending the next show on Netflix to managing supply chains in warehouses)

We're not talking about AI that's sentient or self-aware (think HAL 9000 from *2001: A Space Odyssey*). Most AI systems today are **narrow AI** — designed to perform specific tasks like translating languages, detecting fraud, or predicting stock prices.

Over the last decade, advances in **machine learning** (a subset of AI) have revolutionized this field. Machine learning enables AI systems to learn from data and improve over time without being explicitly programmed to do so. This means AI systems can get smarter with experience, often becoming better than humans at performing tasks.

AI's role in our lives isn't just limited to "smart" devices or digital assistants. AI is beginning to impact industries, economies, and entire job markets in ways that are both exciting and intimidating. Your understanding of how these developments are unfolding is critical to avoid getting left behind.

AI's Growing Presence in Everyday Life

You might not think of yourself as "living in an AI world," but look around. It's likely that almost every part of your day already involves AI in some capacity:

- **Social Media:** AI algorithms determine the posts you see on Instagram, Facebook, and TikTok, tailoring your feed to what it thinks will keep you engaged. The more you interact, the better the system gets at understanding what you like.

- **Healthcare:** AI-driven tools help doctors analyze medical images, diagnose diseases, and even predict patient outcomes. Some apps use AI to monitor your health by tracking your diet, exercise, or even mental well-being.

- **Finance:** Banks use AI to detect fraud by analyzing spending patterns and flagging any suspicious activity. AI is also used for investment strategies, portfolio management, and even to determine your creditworthiness.

- **Entertainment:** Netflix, Spotify, and YouTube all rely on AI to recommend content based on your preferences, viewing history, and engagement.

This is just the beginning. AI is poised to permeate even more areas of life — from autonomous vehicles to personalized education to advanced manufacturing. And as AI becomes more advanced, it's likely that its presence will only increase.

The Role of AI in the Economy and Job Market

AI is already reshaping the global economy. In the workplace, it's driving productivity, innovation, and efficiency. AI also raises critical questions about the future of work:

- **Automation of Repetitive Tasks:** For years, companies have used technology to automate basic tasks, but AI is furthering this initiative. Jobs that rely heavily on repetitive actions or basic decision-making are at risk of being automated. For example, customer service jobs are increasingly being replaced by AI chatbots, while industries like manufacturing are seeing the rise of robots that can assemble products with high precision.

- **AI-Augmented Jobs:** AI is also changing jobs by **augmenting** what people do. Instead of completely replacing workers, AI is being used to assist and enhance human abilities. For instance, an architect might use AI tools to design buildings more efficiently, while a doctor could leverage AI-powered diagnostic tools to assist in decision-making. AI doesn't necessarily replace the worker, but rather shifts the tasks and skills required for the role.
- **Emerging Jobs:** New careers are being created as a direct result of AI, many of which didn't exist even a decade ago. Roles like AI specialists, data scientists, and machine learning engineers are in high demand. These are the people who design, develop, and implement AI systems.

However, the challenge lies in the fact that AI is also expected to displace millions of jobs in certain sectors. A 2023 report from the World Economic Forum predicted that by 2025, AI and automation will displace 85 million jobs globally — though it also noted that new technology would create 97 million new roles. The question is not whether AI will change the job market — it's how you, as an older Millennial, can navigate this disruption.

AI in Industry: Transforming Everything

AI's influence is spreading to every industry, reshaping how businesses operate, make decisions, and deliver products and services. Let's look at how some key industries are being impacted:

- **Healthcare:** AI-powered diagnostics, treatment recommendations, and even drug discovery are transforming the healthcare sector. AI systems can now help doctors diagnose diseases like cancer and diabetes more accurately by analyzing medical images or genetic data. Some AI programs can even detect early signs of diseases like Alzheimer's before symptoms appear.

- **Retail and E-commerce:** AI is used to track purchasing behavior and predict future trends. Think about how Amazon recommends products you might like based on previous purchases — that's AI in action. In physical stores, AI-powered cameras and sensors help track inventory levels and optimize product placement, improving the overall shopping experience.

- **Finance:** Banks and financial institutions are leveraging AI to detect fraud, predict stock market trends, and manage risk. In addition, AI is used in algorithmic trading to make high-frequency trades that outperform human traders. As AI continues to evolve, it's expected to play an even larger role in wealth management and financial planning.

- **Transportation and Logistics:** Self-driving cars, drones, and AI-powered logistics systems are set to revolutionize the transportation industry. For example, AI is already being used in route optimization and autonomous delivery vehicles, saving companies time and money. While fully autonomous vehicles are still being tested, AI has the potential to drastically change everything from public transport to freight delivery.

What Does This Mean for You?

The AI revolution is here — but how does this impact you, as someone who grew up in the pre-AI world? The rapid pace of AI development can feel overwhelming. In some ways, it might seem like AI is moving too fast for anyone to catch up. But here's the key takeaway: understanding AI and its implications doesn't mean you need to become an expert in the technology itself. Instead, it's about **being aware** of how AI is affecting the world around you, especially in your career and personal life.

AI is not just for tech companies or sci-fi enthusiasts. It's increasingly embedded in industries you already work in, whether that's marketing, education, healthcare, or business. AI is a tool that can help improve efficiency, create new products and services, and open up new markets. But if you're not aware of how these changes are unfolding, you might miss out on opportunities to leverage AI for your benefit.

The good news is that, as an older Millennial, you have the advantage of experience and adaptability. While AI might change the tools and methods you use in your job, it can't replace the judgment, emotional intelligence, and creativity that you bring to your work. The key is to understand how AI will affect your industry and how you can integrate it into your skill set — whether it's through learning how to use AI tools or shifting to new roles that AI is creating.

The Next Step: Understanding AI's Impact on You

Now that we've covered the basics, it's time to think critically about how AI will affect your career, lifestyle, and future. In the next chapter, we'll dive deeper into the specific risks and opportunities that older Millennials face in the age of AI. Take a moment to reflect on how AI is already present in your life. What technologies do you use every day? Where could AI potentially improve your productivity or creativity?

By understanding AI now, you can begin to adapt — not just to survive, but to thrive in the future of work.

Chapter 2: The Risk of Falling Behind: Why Millennials Are At a Crossroads

As an older Millennial, you're in a challenging position. Unlike Gen Z, who is growing up with AI as a part of their everyday life, you didn't grow up in a digital-first world. Sure, you remember dial-up internet and using floppy disks, but now you're being asked to compete with younger generations who are digital natives.

The challenge is real, but it's also a massive opportunity. As AI transforms industries, those who fail to adapt run the risk of being left behind. Whether it's automation displacing jobs, or the rise of AI-driven decision-making, the landscape of work and life is shifting.

But here's the good news: Millennials are known for being adaptable, creative, and resourceful. These traits will serve you well in the age of AI.

A Generation in Transition

Millennials (born roughly between 1981 and 1996) are the last generation that can remember a time before smartphones, social media, and the internet. Many of us had to learn how to adapt as the digital world grew around us, while also navigating the traditional "pre-tech" systems that our parents had relied on. We were the first generation to really experience the transition from analog to digital, and that gives us a unique set of skills. We were also the last group that entered the workforce largely without the influence of AI, automation, and constant connectivity.

We now face a unique crossroads. We're not exactly "digital natives" like Gen Z, who grew up in a world where AI, machine learning, and automation were already a part of daily life. At the same time, we're not "baby boomers" who are transitioning to retirement. We're in the prime of our careers and lives, and that puts us at a critical juncture in a world being reshaped by AI.

The question is: how do we continue to thrive in a world that's changing faster than ever? And how do we avoid the risk of becoming obsolete?

The Speed of Change: How AI Is Reshaping Everything

One of the biggest challenges we face as older Millennials is that we've watched technology change at an exponential rate. What once felt like a slow evolution — think back to the early days of the internet or the first iPhone — has now accelerated beyond our control. AI, which was once the stuff of science fiction, is now a core part of many industries, from healthcare to finance to manufacturing.

While we were busy perfecting the art of sending the perfect email, other generations were growing up coding, building apps, and learning how to build complex AI systems. This has created a significant generational gap when it comes to the workforce. According to reports, many of the jobs that existed when we started our careers are already being automated — and more will soon follow.

It's not just the traditional "low-skill" jobs that AI threatens. Many "white-collar" roles — such as those in accounting, data entry, customer service, and even management — are increasingly being replaced by AI-driven processes. AI's ability to analyze massive datasets and execute routine tasks faster than humans has led companies to rethink and reshape their workforce strategies.

For older Millennials, this means two things:

1. **Job Displacement:** Certain jobs we've relied on — or even specialized in — may disappear or be dramatically transformed by automation. Think about how AI-powered customer service chatbots are replacing traditional call center workers or how AI-driven algorithms are helping businesses make investment decisions, leaving financial advisors to focus on more complex tasks.
2. **Skill Gap:** The speed of change means that the skills we gained during our formal education, early career, or previous jobs might no longer be sufficient. If we're not actively adapting, the gap between the skills we have and those needed in the workforce will only widen.

Why Millennials Are Particularly Vulnerable

At first glance, it may seem like Millennials would be well-positioned to thrive in this new AI-powered world. After all, we grew up with the internet and technology. But the truth is, Millennials find themselves at a unique disadvantage in several ways:

1. **The Transition from Old to New:** As mentioned, Millennials were raised in a world where tech was evolving rapidly, but we didn't grow up with AI in the same way Gen Z has. Many of us came of age in the pre-social media era and had to learn digital skills on the fly. While younger generations may be more adept at using new tools (think generative AI for content creation or advanced data analysis), we may feel like we're playing catch-up.

2. **The Pressure to "Do It All":** Millennials often feel an added layer of stress when it comes to career and personal life. We've been dealing with a challenging economic climate, from the 2008 recession to the rise of gig work and the financial strains of the COVID-19 pandemic. We're facing

the pressure of paying off student loans while trying to secure stable jobs and raise families. This pressure makes it harder to find the time or energy to invest in learning new skills or re-skilling for an AI-driven world.

3. **The "Mid-Career Crisis" of the AI Age**: While many younger workers can easily pivot or change career paths, Millennials often find themselves deeply entrenched in their careers. As we reach mid-career, the idea of "starting over" or shifting industries can feel daunting. On top of that, many Millennials face the prospect of having to continuously "reinvent" themselves in a rapidly changing job market, something previous generations didn't experience as acutely.

4. **The Fear of Being Left Behind**: As AI continues to infiltrate workplaces, it can trigger a sense of insecurity. If your job involves repetitive tasks or routine decision-making, there's a very real fear that AI could do it better, faster, and cheaper. This can lead to anxiety about job stability or even the relevance of your entire career path.

The Silver Lining: Embracing Change and Opportunity

Despite the risks, Millennials are in an excellent position to thrive — provided we make the conscious choice to **adapt** and **embrace change**.

AI doesn't have to be an existential threat. In fact, it can be an ally. For example, AI tools can streamline many administrative tasks, allowing you to focus on higher-level work. AI can also help you make more informed decisions, by providing deep insights into data that would have been nearly impossible to process manually. By learning how to incorporate AI into your existing worflow, you can unlock new productivity and creative potential.

Millennials are often seen as adaptable and resourceful, and these traits are our greatest assets in the AI revolution. While younger generations might have a technological edge, we have valuable experience, leadership qualities, and problem-solving skills that machines can't replicate. Our ability to see the bigger picture, understand nuance, and approach problems creatively means we can continue to deliver value in ways AI cannot — at least not yet.

What You Can Do Right Now: Proactive Steps to Stay Ahead

The first step in adapting to the AI-driven world is to **acknowledge** that change is happening and that you don't have to be afraid of it. The future isn't something that happens to you — it's something you actively participate in shaping.

Here are some strategies to stay ahead:

1. **Learn the Basics of AI**: Don't be intimidated by AI jargon. You don't need to become an AI expert, but learning the fundamentals — like how AI works, how machine learning differs from traditional programming, and how AI is being used in your industry — is crucial. There are free online courses, videos, and articles that can help you understand these concepts without needing a tech background. This book is a great start.

2. **Identify AI Tools that Can Help You**: AI is already a part of many tools you probably use daily. From AI-powered personal assistants like Siri and Google Assistant to AI-driven platforms like Grammarly, these tools can make you more productive and efficient. Explore AI in your industry, too — there are AI-driven analytics tools, design software, and customer relationship management (CRM) platforms that can help you perform your job better.

3. **Focus on Skills AI Can't Replace**: While AI may be great at automating tasks and analyzing data, there are certain human skills it simply can't replicate. These include creativity, empathy, and emotional intelligence. Develop and hone skills that emphasize human connection, problem-solving, and strategic thinking. These are qualities that will remain in demand, even in an AI-driven world.

4. **Consider Upskilling or Reskilling**: As AI continues to evolve, so will the types of skills that are in demand. Focus on acquiring skills that complement AI, such as learning how to work with AI tools, improving your data literacy, or understanding how AI impacts your specific field. This could involve taking online courses, attending workshops, or even earning certifications in data science or AI.

5. **Shift to Roles Where AI Assists, Not Replaces**: In many industries, AI is an assistant, not a replacement. Consider roles where AI can enhance your productivity — from working alongside AI to improve decision-making, to using AI to generate insights in marketing or finance. By focusing on jobs that require human intelligence, you can avoid roles that AI is likely to automate.

The Future is Not Set in Stone

In the end, the risk of falling behind isn't as much about the threat AI poses to your career, but about how you choose to respond to this new reality. It's easy to feel overwhelmed or anxious about the rapid pace of change, but the reality is that the future of work is still in our hands.

As an older Millennial, you have the advantage of a lifetime of experience, the ability to adapt, and the creativity to figure out how to thrive in a world of constant technological change. The key to staying ahead is to keep learning, stay agile, and embrace the opportunities AI brings rather than fearing it.

The future is being built right now — and you have a role to play in shaping it.

Chapter 3: Your Superpower as a Millennial: Leveraging Experience in a World of Automation

Here's something that's easy to overlook: You have something extremely powerful and valuable that younger generations don't. Experience. While Gen Z might be tech-savvy, you've navigated a world of constant change and uncertainty. You've dealt with recessions, shifting job markets, and the rapid evolution of technology. That makes you adaptable — and adaptability is one of the most valuable traits in the AI era.

AI is great at processing data and automating tasks, but it still can't replicate the super powers of human touch, insight, creativity, and emotional intelligence that you bring to the table. While AI may replace certain types of jobs, it can't replace your depth of experience, your ability to solve problems, and your capacity to connect with others on a human level.

The Value of Experience in a Changing World

In the age of automation and AI, many younger generations are seen as more "technologically savvy" due to their digital fluency. But here's where the Millennial generation holds a unique advantage: **experience**. While it's true that younger generations might have grown up with the latest tech, Millennials bring something to the table that AI can't replace — **a wealth of real-world experience** and **critical thinking skills** honed through navigating the challenges of life and work.

The Depth of Judgment and Decision-Making

AI can analyze vast amounts of data in seconds, but it lacks the nuanced judgment that comes from experience. While AI can make predictions or suggestions based on data, it's still not capable of understanding the complexities of human interaction or the subtle dynamics of relationships — areas where Millennials excel.

Consider a manager in their mid-30s who has worked their way through entry-level positions, learning to motivate teams, navigate office politics, difficult bosses and make tough decisions in high-pressure environments. AI can provide data on performance metrics, but it can't replace the human touch needed to lead, inspire, or mentor others.

Similarly, in personal life, Millennials often find themselves juggling multiple roles — from caring for children and aging parents to managing personal finances and maintaining a work-life balance. These experiences foster resilience, creativity, and the ability to prioritize — all qualities that AI cannot replicate.

The Power of Human Insight

AI is a powerful tool for processing and analyzing information, but it cannot understand the context in which that information is being used. For example, in creative fields like writing, design, or advertising, AI might generate content or suggest layouts, but it can't offer the same intuitive understanding of cultural trends, emotional nuance, or the subtleties of human storytelling that someone with years of professional experience brings to the table.

Millennials who have worked in customer service, project management, or any collaborative role can apply their **empathy, interpersonal skills**, and **problem-solving** abilities in ways that AI simply cannot. They understand the importance of reading body language, responding to emotional cues, and adjusting communication styles based on individual needs — something that's especially critical in leadership and client-facing roles.

Millennial Strengths: Adaptability and Innovation

One of the greatest strengths of Millennials is our ability to adapt to new technologies, methods, and ways of thinking. We've lived through several major technological shifts: the rise of the internet, the advent of smartphones, the boom of social media, and now the AI revolution. Unlike Baby Boomers, who might find the pace of change overwhelming, and Gen Z, who may not have experienced life before technology, we've lived through **both worlds**.

Adaptability in the Face of Change

Millennials are often described as the "adaptable" generation. We've had to constantly reinvent ourselves, from navigating the gig economy to pivoting careers during recessions or shifting to remote work during the pandemic. We've learned how to embrace change because we've had no other choice. Now, this ability to evolve will be a crucial asset in the world of AI.

For example, a Millennial working in retail might have started in a customer-facing position, then adapted to using advanced point-of-sale (POS) systems, learned how to manage online orders, and may even have shifted to roles focused on digital marketing or e-commerce. This transition from "brick-and-mortar" retail to e-commerce is just one example of how Millennials have continuously upskilled to meet the demands of the digital world. This same mindset can be applied to adapting to the AI-powered job market.

Innovation in Problem-Solving

AI and automation excel at solving structured, repetitive problems, but they can't innovate. The **human touch** — the ability to approach challenges with creativity and fresh perspectives — is what sets Millennials apart in the workplace. The tech-savvy, entrepreneurial spirit of the Millennial generation can fuel innovation, and AI can serve as a valuable tool to augment this process, not replace it.

Take, for instance, a Millennial marketing professional who is tasked with increasing brand engagement. AI tools can help analyze audience data and suggest strategies, but it's the Millennial marketer's creativity that will determine the campaign's direction. They can combine data insights with a unique vision to create content that resonates with audiences, experiment with new formats like TikTok videos or interactive stories, and pivot when something doesn't work — all skills that are still rooted in human ingenuity.

As AI takes over more technical tasks, **Millennials have the chance to focus on areas where human ingenuity is key**: refining ideas, thinking outside the box, and introducing creative solutions. AI can streamline and optimize; humans bring the **vision** and **strategy**.

Becoming a "Human-AI Hybrid"

While many fear that AI will replace their jobs, the real opportunity lies in **working alongside AI**. Rather than seeing AI as a threat, Millennials can embrace it as a **partner** to enhance their abilities, improve efficiency, and unlock new creative possibilities.

How to Work with AI

AI is not just for programmers, engineers, or data scientists. Many industries are already implementing AI tools that are accessible to people with a variety of skill sets. If you're in a creative role, AI tools like **GPT-4** (for content creation) or **Canva's AI design assistant** can help you brainstorm ideas, automate mundane tasks (like resizing images), and generate drafts, allowing you to focus on higher-level strategy.

For professionals in finance, tools like **Kensho** (for financial analysis) or **Robo-Advisors** can process data and suggest investment strategies, but it takes human oversight to determine whether these strategies align with personal goals or ethical standards. The same goes for healthcare, where AI-driven diagnostic tools can help identify patterns in medical images, but doctors still bring **critical thinking** and **human care** to patient interactions.

The key to success in the future of work is becoming a "human-AI hybrid." Here's how to cultivate that mindset:

- **Use AI to Handle Repetitive Tasks:** If your job involves a lot of administrative or repetitive tasks, AI tools can help streamline your workflow. For example, AI-powered scheduling tools like **x.ai** can manage your calendar, while AI-driven customer service platforms (e.g., **Zendesk** or **Intercom**) can handle initial queries.

- **Enhance Your Skills with AI:** As a professional, understanding how to incorporate AI into your workflow can make you more valuable to employers. Whether it's automating data entry or using AI-driven design tools, learning how to integrate AI into your day-to-day activities can save you time and increase productivity.

- **Develop Emotional Intelligence (EI) & Leadership Skills:** While AI can analyze data and automate tasks, it can't replicate **emotional intelligence** or **leadership abilities**. Cultivate your capacity for empathy, communication, and decision-making to become an irreplaceable leader in the workplace.

The Future of Work: AI as a Tool, Not a Replacement

In an AI-powered world, Millennials have the opportunity to **guide AI** rather than be overtaken by it. For example, roles like **AI ethicists**, **AI project managers**, and **AI product designers** are emerging, requiring both technological literacy and deep understanding of human needs, biases, and societal impact.

Millennials who have experience in project management or consulting can find these roles appealing — they already possess the leadership, communication, and organizational skills needed to oversee AI projects. Their role will be to integrate AI into workflows, manage the ethical implications, and ensure that AI tools align with human values.

Leading Teams in an AI-Driven Environment

As AI becomes more integrated into the workplace, there's a rising demand for **AI-savvy leaders** who can guide teams through this transition. Millennials, with their hands-on experience in tech adoption and ability to manage cross-functional teams, are well-positioned to take on these leadership roles.

Building AI-Ready Teams

Leading a team in the AI era means being able to both understand the technology and effectively manage people who may not be familiar with it. Millennials can leverage their **communication skills** and **empathy** to educate and support their teams as AI tools are introduced.

- **Fostering a Growth Mindset:** Help your team see AI as an opportunity to grow rather than as a job killer. Encourage them to see AI as an augmentation of their skills, not a replacement. This mindset shift can help ease any fears your team may have about automation.

- **Investing in Learning and Development:** Encourage continuous learning within your team. Offer resources and opportunities for professional development to help team members stay ahead of the curve, whether that's learning new AI tools, taking up courses on data analytics, or simply staying updated on industry trends.

Leading with Vision in an AI Era

As AI handles more of the operational and data-heavy tasks, your role as a leader will focus more on **vision** and **strategy**. How do you align AI tools with your company's mission? How can AI help solve the company's long-term challenges? Your role will evolve to one of guiding your team through technological change and leading them with purpose in an AI-enhanced world.

The Future Is Human + AI

As AI continues to evolve, Millennials will face increasing pressure to adapt to a rapidly changing world. But with the right mindset and the strategic use of AI tools, Millennials can not only keep up with these changes but also **thrive** in them.

The true power of AI lies in its ability to enhance and amplify human capabilities. By embracing the opportunities AI presents, Millennials can harness their unique blend of experience,

Chapter 4: Getting Comfortable with Change: Embracing Lifelong Learning

The key to staying ahead in a world of constant change is learning. Here's the reality: AI won't stop advancing, so neither can your learning. The good news is that learning doesn't have to mean going back to school for another degree. There are countless resources — from online courses to podcasts to webinars — that can help you keep your skills sharp.

This chapter focuses on how to cultivate a mindset of lifelong learning. We'll explore strategies for staying curious, embracing new tools and technologies, and integrating learning into your daily routine.

4.1 The Necessity of Lifelong Learning

As the world accelerates into the AI-driven future, **continuous learning** will become the key differentiator between those who thrive in the age of automation and those who are left behind. The days of learning a single skill set for life are long gone. Millennials must embrace the reality that **learning is no longer optional** — it's a lifelong commitment.

The Accelerating Pace of Change

Every few years, new technology, methodologies, and tools disrupt industries, and AI is one of the most profound of these shifts. When Millennials entered the workforce, technologies like **social media**, **cloud computing**, and **smartphones** were already reshaping industries. Now, AI is fundamentally changing how we live and work. This creates a new challenge: the technology of today could be obsolete in five to ten years.

Unlike previous generations, who might have stayed in one job or industry for decades, Millennials will likely find themselves shifting career paths or working with entirely new tools multiple times throughout their lives. As the landscape of work evolves, so too must the skills and knowledge that drive career success.

The Rise of the "Learning Economy"

In the AI era, knowledge isn't static — it's evolving. The economy is increasingly shaped by the **"learning economy"** — a system where adaptability and the ability to acquire new skills are as important as formal qualifications. In this new economy, it's not enough to simply have a degree or past experience; the ability to continuously update your skillset is what will ensure long-term employability.

Many jobs that existed a decade ago will either disappear or evolve into something unrecognizable. For instance, professions like telemarketers or assembly line workers have been heavily impacted by automation. On the other hand, roles like **AI training specialists**, **data analysts**, and **AI ethicists** are emerging in new industries. To take advantage of these new opportunities, Millennials must **actively seek new knowledge** and not rest on their laurels.

Growth Mindset: Embracing the Challenge

In order to thrive in this ever-changing world, Millennials need to cultivate a **growth mindset** — the belief that skills and intelligence can be developed through effort, learning, and persistence. Those who approach new challenges with curiosity and resilience will be more equipped to handle the rapid advancements in AI and automation.

Having a growth mindset means **seeing challenges as opportunities** to learn, rather than as insurmountable obstacles. For instance, instead of feeling overwhelmed by the idea of learning to work with AI, those with a growth mindset will approach it as an exciting opportunity to develop a new set of tools that will enhance their productivity and creativity.

Developing a Growth Mindset

While it might seem daunting to navigate a world where the pace of change is accelerating, Millennials have a major advantage: **flexibility and resilience**. The ability to adapt quickly and learn on the fly is a skill that can be cultivated, and it's crucial for staying relevant in the AI-powered economy.

Overcoming Fear of Change

A major barrier to learning new skills is the fear of **failure** or the discomfort that comes with stepping outside of your comfort zone. It's easy to feel like AI and other technological changes are beyond our control or comprehension. This fear can paralyze us and prevent us from trying new things. However, overcoming this fear is essential to embracing lifelong learning.

A simple yet effective strategy for overcoming fear is to **reframe failure**. Instead of seeing a failed attempt at learning a new skill as a setback, view it as **feedback**. Every challenge you face is an opportunity to grow. For example, if you struggle to learn a new tool or AI platform, it's not a reflection of your ability but rather a signal that you need more practice. The more you learn and fail, the closer you get to mastery.

The Power of Incremental Progress

A key concept in building a growth mindset is **small, consistent improvements**. The idea of having to master complex AI systems or new tools can seem overwhelming. However, breaking down the learning process into manageable steps can help overcome that feeling of being overwhelmed. Instead of focusing on the end goal, concentrate on the small daily actions that will get you closer to it.

For instance, if you're looking to become proficient in using AI tools for content creation (e.g., text generation software or AI-based design platforms), start with small projects. Focus on using one AI tool at a time, mastering its basic functions, and applying it in a project. Once you're comfortable with the tool, gradually move to more advanced features.

Building Emotional Resilience

Building a growth mindset also involves **developing emotional resilience**. With so much technological disruption, it's natural to experience anxiety and uncertainty. But resilience is about learning to cope with setbacks and seeing failures as part of the learning process.

Mindfulness, **self-compassion**, and **positive self-talk** are all techniques that can help build the mental strength necessary for continuous learning. For example, when feeling frustrated with a new skill, rather than getting discouraged, remind yourself that learning something new always involves a period of discomfort, and that discomfort is a sign you're growing.

Learning How to Learn

In an age where knowledge is expanding rapidly and where the ability to acquire new skills is critical, learning how to learn becomes one of the most valuable skills Millennials can possess. Fortunately, the digital age provides numerous resources to help with this process.

Curating Your Own Learning Journey

One of the great advantages Millennials have in the age of AI is the **access to learning resources**. Gone are the days when formal education was the only option for skill-building. Now, Millennials can access everything from free MOOCs (Massive Open Online Courses) to specialized AI learning platforms.

- **Coursera**, **edX**, and **Udemy** offer a wide range of courses in AI, machine learning, data science, and other in-demand fields. These platforms are designed to cater to learners of all levels, offering beginner courses as well as advanced certifications.

- **YouTube** and **Podcasts**: For a more informal learning experience, YouTube and podcasts offer endless educational content on a wide variety of topics, from coding tutorials to discussions on the ethics of AI.

- **AI-powered learning tools** like **Duolingo** for language learning or **Grammarly** for writing also enable people to learn efficiently in bite-sized chunks.

The key to curating your own learning journey is to start with **clear goals** and stay organized. For instance, if you want to become proficient in using AI for marketing, start with a basic understanding of AI concepts before diving into more specialized tools like Google's **AutoML** or Facebook's AI tools for ad targeting. By structuring your learning and focusing on one aspect at a time, you can avoid overwhelm and steadily improve your skills.

Microlearning: The Future of Skill Acquisition

One of the most effective ways to learn in today's world is through **microlearning** — a process that involves breaking down complex topics into smaller, manageable chunks that can be absorbed in short bursts of time. Microlearning aligns perfectly with the pace of modern life, where time and attention are limited.

For example, you could dedicate just 15-20 minutes a day to learning a new skill, whether it's experimenting with a new AI tool, reading an article on machine learning, or watching a short tutorial on coding. Over time, these short learning sessions add up and compound into significant expertise.

Self-Reflection and Continuous Improvement

One of the most important aspects of lifelong learning is **self-reflection**. Taking the time to reflect on what you've learned, how it can be applied, and where you need to improve allows for a deeper understanding and mastery of the material. Whether you keep a learning journal or engage in reflective practices such as **meditation**, regular self-assessment helps you gauge your progress and identify areas that need further attention.

Practical Steps for Lifelong Learning

Now that we've covered the mindset and strategies for lifelong learning, let's look at some **practical steps** that Millennials can take to stay on top of the AI-driven economy:

1. **Make Learning a Daily Habit**: Set aside time each day to learn something new — even if it's just 10-20 minutes. Consistency is key. Whether it's through reading, watching educational videos, or practicing a new skill, make it a non-negotiable part of your routine.

2. **Identify Core Skills for the Future**: Focus on learning **high-demand skills** such as data literacy, coding (Python, R), AI concepts, and digital marketing. These skills will help you stay relevant in an AI-driven world. As new technologies emerge, pivot your learning to stay ahead of the curve.

3. **Leverage AI for Learning**: Use AI-powered tools that enhance your learning experience. Platforms like **LinkedIn Learning, Khan Academy**, and **Duolingo** use algorithms to recommend courses and content based on your interests and previous learning history, making your educational journey more tailored and efficient.

4. **Join Communities of Learners**: Engage with communities, either online or in-person, where you can share knowledge and experiences. Whether it's a **Reddit forum**, a **LinkedIn group**, or a **local Meetup**, connecting with others who are also learning AI or other relevant skills will help you stay motivated and gain diverse perspectives.

5. **Stay Curious**: Foster a **curiosity-driven approach** to learning. This involves not just acquiring new skills for the sake of career advancement, but developing a genuine interest in how things work and a desire to learn simply for the joy of learning. This mindset will keep you adaptable, inquisitive, and resilient as new technologies emerge.

The Power of Lifelong Learning

The ability to **learn continuously** is a superpower that Millennials possess in the age of AI. The future of work is not just about working alongside robots — it's about constantly evolving to work **with** new technologies in ways that are meaningful and innovative. By adopting a mindset of lifelong learning, Millennials can stay relevant, adaptable, and empowered in a world that is being rapidly transformed by AI and automation.

Chapter 5: Re-Skilling for Relevance: Practical Steps to Stay Ahead

Let's get practical. It's one thing to say you need to learn, but what exactly should you focus on? What skills are most likely to make you indispensable in the age of AI?

This chapter breaks down the key areas where you can upskill to remain competitive. From learning how to work with AI tools to enhancing your communication and leadership skills, we'll cover everything you need to stay relevant and in-demand.

The Changing Landscape of Careers

The rise of AI and automation has already begun to reshape industries, and the future of work will likely look radically different from what we know today. Many Millennials, especially those who entered the workforce in the late 2000s and early 2010s, have already experienced seismic shifts — from the gig economy to the rise of remote work, to the increasing need for digital literacy. Now, AI is adding a new layer of complexity and opportunity.

Job Displacement vs. Job Transformation

One of the biggest concerns surrounding AI is **job displacement**. There's no doubt that certain jobs — particularly those involving routine, repetitive tasks — will be automated. According to studies by McKinsey and the World Economic Forum, jobs like customer service representatives, telemarketers, and certain manufacturing roles are at risk of being replaced by AI systems and robots. This creates understandable fear for many workers who might find themselves suddenly redundant.

However, the more important and optimistic reality is that **AI will not just replace jobs — it will transform them**. Just as the introduction of the internet transformed industries like retail, publishing, and communications, AI will augment and enhance many existing roles. In fact, **new job categories** are already emerging, with positions like **AI trainers**, **data curators**, and **AI ethicists** becoming increasingly in demand.

Millennials have the opportunity to navigate these shifts, not by avoiding them, but by **embracing the transformation** and adapting their careers to meet the changing landscape. The question isn't about whether AI will replace jobs; it's about how Millennials can **transition to new, meaningful roles** that leverage their strengths and take advantage of the technological revolution.

Evolving Roles and the Rise of Hybrid Jobs

The future of work won't consist of a simple division between "human" and "machine" jobs. Instead, **hybrid roles** will become increasingly common. These are jobs that blend human expertise with AI tools, requiring a combination of technical knowledge and human insight.

For example, a **marketing strategist** might use AI to analyze consumer data and predict trends, but it's their creative insight that drives the campaign strategy. Similarly, a **healthcare administrator** might leverage AI-powered scheduling and patient management systems but will still need to communicate with patients, resolve complex cases, and oversee day-to-day operations.

In this new world, Millennials will find themselves increasingly tasked with **combining human skills (creativity, problem-solving, emotional intelligence)** with AI-driven tools. These hybrid jobs may span industries from tech and healthcare to entertainment and education, and Millennials who stay flexible and open to learning will be best positioned to seize these opportunities.

Identifying Future-Proof Skills

While the exact shape of the future job market is still unfolding, there are certain **skills** that will help Millennials stay ahead of the curve. These "future-proof" skills will allow you to adapt to the inevitable changes in your career, making you more resilient, marketable, and indispensable in an AI-powered world.

Technical Literacy

In the world of AI, **technical literacy** doesn't mean you need to become a coder or data scientist. However, understanding the basics of how AI works and how it applies to your field is becoming increasingly essential. Knowing how to use AI tools, manage AI-driven processes, or collaborate with technical teams will give you a major edge.

Skills in **data literacy** will also be crucial. Understanding how to interpret data, recognize patterns, and make data-driven decisions is a skill that will be highly valued across nearly all industries. Whether you work in marketing, finance, healthcare, or customer service, the ability to work with data is critical.

Creativity and Emotional Intelligence (EQ)

While AI is excellent at analyzing patterns and automating tasks, it cannot replicate the complex, emotional, and creative aspects of human work. **Creativity** will be one of the most valuable skills in the AI era, especially as it pertains to solving novel problems, designing new systems, and producing innovative content. As AI takes over routine tasks, there will be an increasing demand for professionals who can bring fresh ideas and innovative solutions.

In tandem with creativity, **emotional intelligence (EQ)** — the ability to recognize and manage your emotions, as well as the emotions of others — will be key to thriving in the AI-driven workplace. AI cannot yet navigate complex interpersonal dynamics, so jobs requiring empathy, leadership, and collaboration will remain highly human-centered. From managing teams to building customer relationships, EQ will be essential for success.

Adaptability and Learning Agility

The most important future-proof skill Millennials can develop is **adaptability** — the ability to continuously learn and evolve with the changing technological landscape. As AI and automation reshape entire industries, the ability to **learn new tools**, **shift careers**, and

pick up new knowledge quickly will be invaluable. The rise of "micro-credentials" and online certifications can offer Millennials the chance to acquire new skills in shorter bursts, without committing to lengthy educational programs.

Transitioning Between Roles: Upskilling and Reskilling

For many Millennials, career transitions will be a central theme of the AI era. The jobs of the past may no longer be viable, but new roles will emerge. Millennials will need to actively **upskill** (add new skills to their existing repertoire) and **reskill** (shift to entirely new skill sets) in order to remain competitive.

The Importance of Upskilling

In the short term, upskilling is a great way to **enhance your current role** without making a drastic change. For instance, if you work in a **customer service** role, learning how to work alongside AI-powered chatbots and automated service systems could help you improve your productivity and serve customers better. Similarly, if you're in **marketing**, becoming proficient in **AI-driven analytics tools** like **Google Analytics**, **HubSpot**, or **Mailchimp's AI capabilities** could make you more effective in campaign management.

Upskilling can often be done with short courses, online certifications, or self-paced learning. It allows you to **remain relevant in your current field** while also expanding your skill set to meet future demands.

The Need for Reskilling

However, for those who see their jobs at risk of automation or those wishing to pursue entirely new careers, **reskilling** will be necessary. This is where Millennials can leverage the tremendous variety of online learning platforms, boot camps, and certification programs available.

If you're a professional in a role that is increasingly automated (e.g., administrative assistants, customer service representatives, etc.), reskilling might mean switching to a different field that's in higher demand, such as:

- **Data science or analytics**
- **Cybersecurity**
- **AI and machine learning (ML)**
- **Digital marketing and e-commerce**
- **Healthcare technology or telemedicine**
- **UX/UI design**

Reskilling often involves gaining **hands-on experience** in a new field, whether through internships, volunteer work, or personal projects. You may need to take on smaller projects to build up a portfolio before fully transitioning to a new career.

Leveraging AI for Reskilling

Ironically, AI itself can help Millennials with their career transitions. AI-driven platforms like **LinkedIn Learning**, **Coursera**, and **Skillshare** offer personalized learning paths based on your current skills and career interests. AI can recommend courses, certifications, and resources tailored to your needs, helping you quickly learn new competencies. These platforms can also guide you through the process of creating a **personalized reskilling plan**, which allows you to make informed decisions about which skills to prioritize.

Creating Career Security in an AI-Driven World

The ultimate question on every Millennial's mind is: **How do I ensure job security in an AI-driven economy?**

While no one can predict exactly what the future holds, there are several strategies Millennials can use to create a stable and secure career, regardless of how the landscape shifts.

Build a Personal Brand

In the age of automation, your **personal brand** can be a key factor in ensuring long-term career security. Establishing yourself as a **thought leader** or **expert** in your field can give you leverage, especially as industries evolve and new technologies emerge. Whether it's by sharing insights on **LinkedIn**, writing articles or blogs, speaking at conferences, or contributing to professional forums, building a personal brand is one of the most effective ways to differentiate yourself from others in the job market.

Diversify Your Skills and Income Streams

In the gig economy, many Millennials are already accustomed to **multiple income streams** — freelancing, side hustles, remote work, or even consulting. The future will likely see even more people working in **hybrid roles** that blend full-time employment with freelance work or entrepreneurial projects. By diversifying your career options and income streams, you'll create a safety net that can help weather economic disruptions caused by automation or market shifts.

- **Freelance work** in areas like writing, design, marketing, or content creation

- **Online courses and coaching** in your area of expertise

- **Remote consulting** for businesses transitioning to AI tools

By continually expanding and diversifying your skill set, you increase your value to the marketplace and create opportunities that can provide greater job security.

Stay Agile: Embrace Career Flexibility

Finally, career **agility** — the ability to quickly pivot or adjust to new roles or industries — will be essential. Millennials who are **flexible** and willing to **adapt to new opportunities** will continue to succeed in the face of AI and automation. The idea of staying in one job or role for life is quickly fading, and those who can transition between

Finally, career **agility** — the ability to quickly pivot or adjust to new roles or industries — will be essential. Millennials who are **flexible** and willing to **adapt to new opportunities** will continue to succeed in the face of AI and automation. The idea of staying in one job or role for life is quickly fading, and those who can transition between roles with ease, learn new skills on the fly, and remain open to change will be best positioned to thrive in the AI-driven economy.

Redefining Success in the Age of AI

In the future of work, the path to success won't be linear. Career shifts, new roles, and job transformation will be commonplace. Millennials must embrace the reality of change, **upskill**, **reskill**, and create new opportunities for themselves as the AI landscape evolves. By staying adaptable, developing a wide range of skills, and being proactive about career growth, Millennials can not only **survive** the changes brought by AI but also **thrive** in them.

Chapter 6: Navigating Your Career in an AI-Driven Economy

AI is changing the way we work. Some jobs will disappear, but new ones will emerge. So how do you navigate this shift?

This chapter helps you rethink your career path and adapt to an economy where the demand for certain roles is changing. Whether it's pivoting to a new industry, embracing freelance work, or finding ways to work alongside AI, we'll discuss strategies for navigating a rapidly evolving job market.

The Ethical Challenges of AI

As Artificial Intelligence becomes increasingly integrated into every aspect of our lives — from healthcare and finance to entertainment and social media — it raises profound ethical questions. These questions are not just for policymakers and tech companies to answer. **Millennials**, as the generation most familiar with the implications of technology on daily life, will need to play an active role in shaping the ethical landscape of AI.

The ethical considerations of AI are complex, as they involve not just technological concerns, but also deeply rooted societal, cultural, and philosophical issues. AI has the potential to do a great deal of good, but it also has the potential to cause harm. Ensuring that AI's influence is positive requires ongoing scrutiny, thoughtful design, and a proactive approach to addressing risks as they arise.

Bias in AI: A Growing Concern

One of the most significant ethical issues with AI is the question of **bias**. AI systems are trained on data — large datasets that often reflect existing societal biases. These biases can be inadvertently encoded into AI algorithms, leading to discriminatory outcomes.

For example, an AI used in hiring might prioritize certain characteristics (such as gender, race, or education level) over others, simply because the historical data used to train it reflected bias. This could result in certain groups being unfairly excluded or marginalized. A well-documented case is the bias in facial recognition technology, which has shown to be less accurate for people of color and women.

The **ethical challenge** here is twofold: ensuring that AI systems are as unbiased and fair as possible, and preventing harmful discrimination that can arise from unexamined data practices.

Data Privacy and Surveillance

Another ethical dilemma is the use of AI in **data collection and surveillance**. With AI capable of analyzing massive amounts of personal data, the lines between **privacy** and **surveillance** are becoming increasingly blurred. AI-powered systems are able to track online behavior, predict personal preferences, and even profile individuals for targeted marketing or law enforcement purposes.

As AI companies collect and monetize data, questions of **ownership** and **consent** arise. Who owns the data generated by individuals? How can people retain control over their digital identities and ensure that their data isn't being used against them or sold without their consent?

Furthermore, AI's role in government surveillance raises significant ethical concerns about the **balance between security and individual freedom**. Governments are increasingly turning to AI for surveillance purposes, but the risk is that AI systems can be used to **infringe upon civil liberties**, such as monitoring political protests or tracking individuals without probable cause.

Autonomous Systems and Accountability

As AI systems become more autonomous — with self-driving cars, robots, and AI decision-making tools — it raises another ethical concern: **accountability**. When AI makes a mistake, who is responsible? If a self-driving car causes an accident, should the manufacturer be held accountable, or should the person who owns the car be liable? When an AI system makes a wrong decision in a medical or financial context, who bears the responsibility?

The issue of **accountability** is crucial because AI systems often operate in **complex, unpredictable environments**, and their decisions might not be easily understood by humans. This "black box" nature of AI makes it difficult to trace how decisions are made, let alone assign responsibility. As AI continues to make decisions on behalf of humans, developing clear frameworks of responsibility will be essential to protecting individuals from harm and ensuring transparency.

Millennials' Role in Ethical AI Development

Millennials have a unique opportunity to shape the future of AI, both in their personal and professional lives. As the first generation to grow up with the internet and smartphones, they are more tech-savvy and aware of the implications of digital technologies than any generation before them. But with this knowledge comes **responsibility**. Millennials are at the forefront of driving change, and as they become the leaders of tomorrow's workforce, they will be the ones who must tackle these ethical issues head-on.

Advocating for Diversity and Inclusion in AI

One of the key ways Millennials can help address bias in AI is by advocating for **diverse and inclusive teams** in AI development. Diverse teams — in terms of gender, race, socio-economic background, and experience — are more likely to create more balanced, fair AI systems. As the AI industry grows, it is essential to bring in perspectives that have historically been marginalized, particularly those that AI technology might disproportionately impact.

Millennials in tech, business, and other industries must prioritize **inclusive hiring practices** and **collaborative environments** that bring together people with different experiences and viewpoints. As workers in various industries, Millennials must also advocate for AI tools that are **designed with fairness** and inclusivity in mind. This can be done by:

- Supporting AI companies that prioritize **ethical design**.

- Pushing for transparency in how AI systems are trained and how data is collected.
- Encouraging AI developers to address **representation gaps** in their data and models.

Supporting Responsible AI Regulations

AI is advancing faster than regulatory frameworks can keep up. Governments and regulatory bodies worldwide are struggling to create legislation that can address the ethical concerns of AI without stifling innovation. Millennials, as future leaders and policymakers, can play a key role in advocating for responsible AI regulations.

Millennials can encourage governments to:

- **Establish clear guidelines** for AI ethics and fairness, particularly when it comes to areas like data privacy, bias, and accountability.
- Promote policies that protect **individual rights** without hindering technological innovation.

- Call for **global collaboration** in regulating AI, given its cross-border nature. Ethical AI should be a **global priority**, and working with international organizations and governments will help set consistent standards.

Millennials can also **push for AI education** in public policy schools, business schools, and other professional settings, helping the next generation of decision-makers understand the complexities of AI technologies and their societal impact.

Building Transparent and Accountable AI Systems

Transparency and accountability are key components in ethical AI. Millennials can push for the development of AI systems that are not just powerful but also explainable. **Explainability** — the ability to understand and trace how an AI arrived at a decision — is crucial for ensuring that AI systems are not operating in a "black box." This will be essential in sectors like healthcare, finance, and criminal justice, where mistakes can have serious consequences.

Millennials can advocate for AI companies and organizations to adopt transparent practices in AI development, including:

- **Clear documentation** of how AI models are trained, including the data sources used and any potential biases that may exist.

- Regular **audits** of AI algorithms to ensure that they align with ethical standards and do not inadvertently perpetuate harm.

- Promoting open-source AI projects that allow the public to scrutinize and understand how algorithms work.

Millennials can also support **ethical AI startups** and organizations that prioritize values such as transparency, equity, and fairness. By doing so, they create a marketplace that rewards ethical behavior and encourages companies to integrate ethical considerations into their design processes.

Ethical AI in Everyday Life: Personal Responsibility

AI isn't just something that exists in the world of tech companies and governments. It's becoming embedded in everyday life. From the **recommendation algorithms** that shape our social media feeds to the AI-driven customer service bots that assist us with issues, AI influences decisions we make and interactions we have on a daily basis.

Ethical Consumption of AI

As consumers, Millennials can adopt an **ethical approach to AI** by being mindful of how they engage with AI-driven products and services. Some of the key actions Millennials can take include:

- **Choosing AI tools and platforms** that prioritize data privacy, fairness, and transparency.

- **Being cautious about personal data sharing**, particularly on social media platforms or apps that use AI for targeted advertising. Understanding how personal data is collected, stored, and used can help Millennials make more informed decisions.

- **Supporting companies that promote ethical AI** and hold themselves accountable to ethical standards. Millennials can vote with their wallets, rewarding businesses that prioritize human well-being over profit.

Advocating for Ethical AI in Education

In addition to consumer responsibility, Millennials can also advocate for **ethical AI education** in schools, universities, and workplaces. AI education should be a critical part of the curriculum, especially for those entering industries like healthcare, law, journalism, and the arts, where AI decisions will have a direct impact on people's lives.

- **Educating future leaders** about the ethical implications of AI will empower them to create better policies, practices, and systems.

- **Encouraging students** to engage with AI not only as a technological tool but also as a **moral and philosophical challenge** will shape a generation of AI practitioners who consider the societal impact of their work.

Shaping the Future with Ethical AI

As AI becomes a central part of modern life, its ethical implications will only continue to grow. Millennials, who are most attuned to the capabilities and risks of AI, must take an active role in shaping its future. By advocating for **responsibility, transparency**, and **inclusivity**, Millennials can help ensure that AI becomes a tool for positive social change rather than a force of harm.

Through **collaboration, education, and engagement**, Millennials can influence AI development, ensuring that it serves humanity as a whole — equitably, transparently, and ethically. It's not just about the technologies we create, but the world we want to live in — a world where AI amplifies human potential and solves the problems that matter most to us, rather than creating new ethical dilemmas or perpetuating injustice.

Chapter 7: The Side Hustle Evolution: AI Tools for Entrepreneurs

AI is also changing the way we approach entrepreneurship. Gone are the days when starting a business required a huge upfront investment in office space, staff, and other resources. Now, AI-powered tools can help you launch and grow your own business with minimal capital.

This chapter explores how older Millennials can use AI to power side hustles, from using AI-driven marketing tools to automating administrative tasks. Whether you want to build an online store, offer consulting services, or create digital products, AI can help you get there faster and smarter.

The Opportunity for Personal Transformation

In a world where AI is revolutionizing everything from healthcare to education, work to social interactions, one of the most powerful opportunities for Millennials is the potential to **harness AI for personal growth**. While AI is often seen as a tool for business efficiency or automation, it can also be an invaluable resource for individuals looking to **optimize their lives**, learn new skills, improve their mental health, and ultimately empower themselves to lead more fulfilling, productive, and innovative lives.

The key to this transformation is understanding that **AI isn't just a replacement for jobs or a tool for corporations**; it can be an incredible personal ally, helping you to navigate the complexities of modern life. By learning how to integrate AI into your daily routines, your educational journey, and your personal development goals, you can unlock a level of growth that wasn't previously possible.

AI as a Personal Coach

One of the most exciting developments in AI is its ability to act as a **personal coach** or mentor. AI tools are now available that can help individuals set and track personal goals, create customized learning plans, and offer ongoing feedback. For instance, platforms like **Noom** for health coaching, **Headspace** for meditation, and even **Duolingo** for language learning leverage AI to create tailored experiences that adjust based on user progress and behavior.

Millennials can use these AI tools to enhance their **physical health**, **mental well-being**, and **skills development**. With AI-driven coaching, you can get personalized recommendations, real-time feedback, and even motivation that adapts to your needs. These tools don't just serve as passive resources; they're proactive, offering insights that might not be immediately obvious but are designed to help you **achieve your full potential**.

Using AI to Boost Productivity and Time Management

For many Millennials, **time management** and **productivity** are central to both career success and personal well-being. AI offers a vast array of tools that can help you work more efficiently, prioritize effectively, and free up time for the things that truly matter.

AI-Powered Personal Assistants

The rise of virtual assistants like **Google Assistant**, **Siri**, and **Amazon Alexa** can significantly improve your productivity by handling simple tasks like scheduling, reminders, or managing emails. These tools can also integrate with your calendar, organize your to-do lists, and automate basic administrative tasks, allowing you to focus on high-level thinking and more complex decision-making.

For Millennials, using a personal assistant to manage appointments, answer queries, and even coordinate work tasks is a time-saver that can reduce mental clutter and improve focus. But the real magic happens when you use these tools in combination with other AI-driven productivity apps.

AI for Task Management

Advanced task management tools like **Trello**, **Notion**, and **Monday.com** are increasingly incorporating AI to help with prioritizing tasks, assigning deadlines, and tracking progress. These tools can analyze your work habits, project timelines, and task dependencies to provide **data-driven recommendations** on how to streamline your workflow and improve your productivity.

AI can also be a huge help in **automating repetitive tasks**, such as responding to common emails, generating reports, or organizing documents. By freeing up time spent on mundane tasks, AI helps Millennials focus on high-value activities, both in their careers and personal lives.

AI for Time Optimization

AI-based apps like **RescueTime** or **Focus@Will** track your digital behavior and offer personalized insights into where you're spending your time. These tools analyze your habits and suggest ways to minimize distractions or optimize your time, ensuring you spend more of it on the things that matter. This can be particularly valuable for Millennials juggling side hustles, full-time jobs, and personal lives, as it helps them strike the delicate balance between work and rest.

By leveraging AI tools designed for productivity, Millennials can maximize their time and get more done without burning out, ensuring that work and personal development remain **aligned** with their long-term goals.

Enhancing Learning and Skill Development

Millennials, often referred to as the **learning generation**, are keenly aware that continuous personal and professional growth is essential for staying relevant in an increasingly competitive world. AI is a powerful tool for enhancing learning experiences, offering customized learning paths, and delivering knowledge in ways that cater to individual learning styles.

AI-Driven Learning Platforms

One of the most exciting ways AI can empower Millennials is through **adaptive learning platforms**. Services like **Coursera, edX,** and **Udemy** use AI to tailor courses and content based on learners' behavior, skill gaps, and interests. These platforms can adjust the difficulty of course materials, provide personalized feedback, and even suggest new areas of study that could help further your career or personal interests.

For example, if you're learning to code, an AI-powered platform can assess where you struggle and automatically adjust the course to give you more practice on those specific concepts. This **adaptive learning technology** ensures that no one is left behind, even if they are starting from scratch or transitioning into a new field.

AI for Lifelong Learning

Lifelong learning is no longer limited to formal education or professional development courses. AI can help Millennials engage in **continuous learning** through everyday interactions. For instance, using AI to read **news summaries** or watch educational **videos** tailored to your interests is an easy way to stay updated and gain new perspectives without spending hours on research.

The ability to **personalize your learning journey** based on your goals and time constraints ensures that every learning experience is efficient and engaging. AI also offers more flexible ways to learn, whether it's through **micro-learning** (small, digestible lessons) or self-paced courses that you can fit into your schedule.

Skill Development for the Future

AI also helps Millennials keep up with **emerging skills** that are essential in the future of work. Whether it's learning **data science**, **machine learning**, **digital marketing**, or **remote collaboration**, AI tools can provide practical guidance and hands-on experiences that accelerate learning.

For example, platforms like **Khan Academy**, **Codecademy**, and **Skillshare** provide personalized learning experiences with AI-curated courses that teach in-demand skills. As the job market continues to evolve and industries undergo massive transformations due to automation and AI, Millennials who take advantage of these learning tools will be better equipped to thrive in new roles and industries.

Using AI for Health and Wellness

The intersection of AI and **healthcare** is one of the most transformative areas for Millennials. As health and wellness become top priorities for this generation, AI can provide tailored solutions for everything from fitness routines to mental health care.

AI for Physical Health

Fitness apps like **MyFitnessPal**, **Fitbit**, and **Peloton** now use AI to analyze your workouts, eating habits, and overall activity levels to deliver customized fitness plans. These AI-powered platforms adjust in real-time based on your progress, making sure you remain challenged while also allowing for recovery. Whether you're training for a marathon or simply aiming to stay in shape, AI can ensure your fitness journey is both **efficient** and **effective**.

AI also plays a role in **health tracking**, where wearables collect data on sleep patterns, heart rate, steps, and other vital statistics. Using this data, AI tools can provide actionable insights into your overall health, help you optimize your sleep schedule, and even predict potential health issues before they arise.

AI for Mental Health

Mental health is an area where AI is also showing immense potential. Chatbots like **Woebot** and **Wysa** provide AI-powered support for individuals dealing with stress, anxiety, and depression. These tools use Cognitive Behavioral Therapy (CBT) techniques to help users manage their emotions and develop healthier coping strategies.

Moreover, AI apps can track mood patterns and offer personalized advice for **stress reduction**, **self-care**, and **mindfulness**, helping individuals build resilience against everyday challenges. By providing real-time emotional support and personalized mental health plans, AI is playing a key role in **democratizing mental wellness** for Millennials.

AI for Nutrition

Personalized nutrition is another area where AI is making a significant impact. Apps like **Eat This Much** use AI to analyze your health goals, preferences, and dietary restrictions to generate personalized meal plans. Similarly, platforms like **Nutrino** offer AI-powered food recommendations based on your genetic makeup, lifestyle, and health goals, allowing for a more **tailored** and **data-driven approach** to nutrition.

AI for Creative Expression and Innovation

Creativity is an essential aspect of personal empowerment, and AI is now being used as a tool for **creative expression** and **innovation**. From generating art and music to assisting with writing and design, AI can act as both a partner and a catalyst for Millennials looking to explore new creative avenues.

AI in Art and Design

Tools like **DALL·E** and **DeepArt** leverage AI to generate images, artwork, and designs based on user input. By simply providing a prompt, users can see AI create stunning visuals, sparking new ideas and possibilities in the creative process.

For Millennials interested in graphic design, illustration, or even web design, AI-powered platforms like **Canva** or **Adobe Sensei** provide suggestions for layouts, color schemes, and typography based on design principles, speeding up the creative process and ensuring professional results.

AI for Music and Writing

AI is also making waves in the music and writing industries. Tools like **Amper Music** and **Aiva** allow creators to generate original music compositions with the help of AI. For writers, platforms like **Grammarly** and **Sudowrite** leverage AI to assist with grammar correction, brainstorming, and even generating content ideas.

AI isn't replacing creativity; rather, it's enhancing it by offering new ways to experiment, iterate, and refine ideas.

Empowering Yourself with AI

The potential of AI to empower Millennials is vast and multifaceted. Whether you're seeking to enhance your career, improve your health, learn new skills, or explore creative outlets, AI offers tools that can accelerate your growth, optimize your time, and provide personalized guidance for every aspect of your life.

To thrive in this new era, Millennials must view AI not just as a tool for business or automation but as a **partner** in personal development. By embracing AI-driven solutions, Millennials can unlock their fullest potential, not just as workers or consumers but as empowered individuals charting their own paths in an ever-evolving world.

The future is one where AI is a tool for **empowerment**, growth, and self-actualization — and the sooner you start integrating it into your life, the sooner you'll be on the path to a more efficient, fulfilling, and innovative future.

Chapter 8: Maintaining Human Connection in an AI-Driven World

One of the biggest concerns with AI is the loss of human connection. As technology automates more and more tasks, will we lose our ability to connect on a personal level? This chapter discusses the importance of maintaining authentic relationships, both personally and professionally, in a world that's increasingly mediated by machines.

AI and the Transformation of Society

As AI continues to evolve, its impact on society will be profound, potentially reshaping everything from community structures to social dynamics. For Millennials, who are already navigating a world of rapid technological change, this transformation presents both challenges and opportunities. AI will not just affect the economy and the workplace, but will also play a major role in redefining our **social systems, relationships**, and even **cultural values**.

The way we interact with others, form relationships, and engage with our communities will be fundamentally altered by AI technologies. The question is: will AI help create a more **inclusive, equitable**, and **connected world**, or will it exacerbate existing divisions and inequalities?

In this chapter, we'll explore how AI is poised to reshape key aspects of society and how Millennials can leverage these changes to foster **meaningful connections, strengthen communities**, and **build a more just and compassionate world**.

AI and the Future of Community Engagement

The concept of "community" has always been central to human life, but in a digital age, that concept is being rapidly redefined. AI can help create new forms of community that transcend physical boundaries, allowing people from diverse backgrounds and geographies to connect in ways that were previously unimaginable.

Digital Communities and Social Platforms

AI-powered platforms like **Facebook**, **Reddit**, and **Discord** already facilitate connections between people with shared interests, regardless of where they live. These platforms use AI algorithms to curate content, making it easier for people to find like-minded individuals and groups. However, this also raises concerns about **echo chambers** and **filter bubbles**, where individuals may be isolated within their own ideological bubbles, reinforcing existing beliefs rather than encountering diverse perspectives.

Millennials have an opportunity to influence how AI shapes these communities. By advocating for **ethical algorithms** and **transparent content moderation**, they can ensure that digital spaces are not only engaging but also inclusive, promoting **positive interaction** and a sense of **belonging**.

AI and Civic Engagement

AI can also be used to enhance **civic engagement** and **democracy**. AI-driven platforms can help citizens become more informed about political issues, track legislation, and facilitate direct communication with policymakers. Tools like **Polis** and **Civiqs** use AI to collect public opinion and identify consensus on key issues, allowing citizens to make their voices heard and influence decision-making processes.

Millennials, who are more likely to be tech-savvy and invested in social change, can use AI to organize campaigns, mobilize voters, and engage in activism. AI-powered tools can help activists identify trends, measure public sentiment, and reach a wider audience, helping them tackle pressing issues like climate change, inequality, and social justice.

Moreover, AI can provide governments with valuable insights into how policies are affecting communities in real time, allowing for more **responsive** and **adaptive governance**. By encouraging the adoption of AI in civic processes, Millennials can help build a more **inclusive**, **participatory democracy**.

AI and the Changing Nature of Relationships

While AI's impact on work and society is well-documented, its effect on personal relationships is often less discussed. AI has the potential to change how we form and maintain relationships, from family dynamics to friendships and romantic partnerships. By understanding these changes, Millennials can proactively shape a future where technology strengthens, rather than replaces, meaningful human connections.

AI in Romantic Relationships

AI is already making its mark in the realm of romantic relationships, particularly through dating apps like **Tinder**, **Bumble**, and **Hinge**, which use AI to match individuals based on shared interests, personality traits, and even **predictive analytics**. These apps are becoming more sophisticated in how they suggest potential partners, with AI learning from user behavior to recommend better matches over time.

However, AI's involvement in dating raises concerns about authenticity and **human connection**. While AI can optimize the process of finding a partner, it cannot replicate the nuanced, emotional, and unpredictable nature of love. Millennials need to remain mindful of this and ensure that while AI may help facilitate connections, it should never replace the **human touch** that is essential for deep, meaningful relationships.

In the future, AI could also play a role in improving existing relationships, including **marriages** and **friendships**. AI-driven apps and tools can help couples or friends track their emotional well-being, provide relationship advice, or offer conflict resolution strategies. For example, apps like **Lasting** or **Couple** use AI to provide couples with personalized communication strategies, helping them nurture their relationships.

AI and Family Dynamics

In families, AI is already transforming how we communicate, organize, and support one another. AI-powered digital assistants like **Amazon Alexa, Google Home**, and **Apple's Siri** are becoming central to home management. These tools help with daily tasks like scheduling, reminders, and even family-oriented entertainment, making it easier for families to stay connected and organized.

Furthermore, AI can enhance **elder care** and help address the challenges faced by an aging population. AI-powered tools can help elderly individuals manage medications, track health data, and even stay mentally engaged through interactive activities. Millennials, who may be caring for aging parents or relatives, can use these technologies to improve quality of life for loved ones.

However, Millennials will need to ensure that these technologies are used **ethically** and do not replace genuine human caregiving. **Human interaction** and **empathy** should remain at the core of any caregiving system, even as AI plays a supporting role.

AI and the Reinvention of Education

Education is one of the areas where AI could have the most significant social impact. The traditional education model, with its reliance on in-person classrooms and rigid curricula, is already being disrupted by online learning platforms, many of which use AI to personalize and adapt the learning experience for each student. But AI's impact on education goes beyond online learning.

Personalized Learning and Equity

AI has the potential to revolutionize **education equity** by providing personalized learning experiences tailored to each student's needs, abilities, and learning styles. Platforms like **Khan Academy** and **Coursera** use AI to adapt lessons and provide real-time feedback. As AI continues to evolve, it could bring an end to the "one-size-fits-all" approach to education, offering tailored, adaptive learning paths that can support learners at every stage of life.

This is particularly important for Millennials who are engaged in **lifelong learning** and may be juggling work, family, and education. AI can help provide flexible, affordable, and personalized learning opportunities that empower individuals to **upskill** and **reskill** without sacrificing their personal or professional lives.

Additionally, AI can support students who have **special learning needs**, helping them access resources and adaptive learning environments that were previously unavailable. By removing barriers to education and providing customized support, AI can contribute to a more **equitable** and **inclusive** educational system.

Redefining Education in a Digital World

AI will also play a role in **redefining education** for a digital world. Beyond traditional subjects, new areas of study like **AI literacy**, **data science**, and **ethics in technology** will become increasingly important. Millennials can help shape the future of education by advocating for curricula that emphasize **critical thinking**, **ethical decision-making**, and **digital citizenship**.

By fostering an understanding of AI's capabilities and limitations, Millennials can ensure that future generations are equipped with the knowledge and skills needed to navigate an AI-driven world. They can also champion the development of **soft skills** — empathy, communication, and creativity — that will remain indispensable, even as automation takes over routine tasks.

AI, Trust, and Social Values

As AI technologies become more embedded in our lives, the issue of **trust** will become increasingly important. Who do we trust to design and deploy AI? What values should AI systems prioritize? And how can we ensure that AI serves the **public good** and promotes social justice?

Trust and Transparency in AI

Transparency in AI systems is critical. **Millennials** need to advocate for **open-source AI** and demand that companies provide clear explanations of how AI algorithms make decisions. In sectors like healthcare, criminal justice, and hiring, the stakes are high, and **biased algorithms** can have devastating consequences. By demanding transparency and accountability, Millennials can help create a world where AI is trusted and used for positive social change.

Ethical AI for Social Good

AI is also poised to help address some of the most pressing challenges facing society today, including climate change, poverty, and inequality. For instance, AI is being used to develop **sustainable technologies**, predict natural disasters, and optimize energy use. **AI for social good** initiatives are already tackling issues like **healthcare accessibility**, **environmental sustainability**, and **disaster relief**, and Millennials can be at the forefront of these efforts.

Millennials can also work to ensure that AI is developed and deployed with a focus on **human dignity**, **equity**, and **social justice**. By advocating for AI that prioritizes the public good and promotes **inclusive values**, Millennials can help build a society where technology is an **ally** in solving humanity's greatest challenges.

Building a Future Together

AI has the potential to fundamentally reshape society — from how we interact with one another to how we learn, work, and engage with our communities. For Millennials, this is both an exciting opportunity and a profound responsibility. By embracing AI with a focus on **ethics, inclusivity**, and **human connection**, Millennials can shape a future where AI serves to **empower individuals**, **strengthen communities**, and create a more **equitable** and **connected world**.

As AI continues to evolve, it is essential that we, as a society, ensure that its development is guided by our deepest values and the needs of **all people**, not just the few. By working together, Millennials can lead the charge in using AI to build a future that reflects the best of what humanity can achieve — a future that is driven by innovation, empathy, and shared responsibility.

Chapter 9: The Mindset Shift: From Fear to Empowerment

Fear is natural when faced with major change, but it can hold you back if you let it. This chapter focuses on shifting your mindset from fear of obsolescence to empowerment in the face of change. With the right perspective, you can see AI as a tool that enhances your capabilities rather than something that threatens your job or your identity.

The Necessity of Adaptability in the Age of AI

Millennials have grown up in a world that has been in constant flux—witnessing the rise of the internet, the proliferation of smartphones, the democratization of information, and the collapse of traditional job structures. But the pace of change we're about to experience as **AI** becomes more integrated into our daily lives is unlike anything we've encountered before. AI's increasing capabilities in automation, creativity, and problem-solving will fundamentally transform the global landscape. However, the ability to **adapt** to these changes is the single most important skill Millennials can cultivate to ensure they thrive.

The world of work, relationships, and even society itself is evolving, and the impact of AI on these areas will be profound. **AI** isn't just a tool; it's a **catalyst for change**. The key to surviving and thriving in this new world is not to resist change, but to **embrace it** and use it to your advantage.

In this chapter, we will explore how Millennials can develop the mindset and skills necessary to **adapt to AI, harness its potential**, and **future-proof** themselves against the uncertainties ahead.

Developing a Growth Mindset in an AI-Driven World

One of the most crucial traits Millennials can adopt in an AI-powered world is a **growth mindset**. Popularized by psychologist Carol Dweck, a growth mindset is the belief that abilities and intelligence can be developed through dedication and hard work. This mindset is crucial as AI disrupts industries and alters how we live and work. Instead of fearing AI as a threat, Millennials should embrace it as an opportunity for **personal growth, learning**, and **reinvention**.

Learning to Love Lifelong Learning

AI will inevitably make some job functions obsolete, but it will also create new industries and roles that didn't exist before. Embracing a growth mindset means committing to **continuous learning**. Millennials who see themselves as **lifelong learners** will be better prepared to capitalize on new opportunities and acquire new skills.

To harness the full potential of AI, Millennials can take the following steps to foster a growth mindset:

- **Adopt an experimental approach**: Instead of fearing failure, treat it as a learning opportunity. AI and automation will change the job landscape, and not every career pivot will go smoothly. But viewing every step of the journey as a learning experience will help you persevere and find your place in this changing world.

- **Embrace change**: The idea of stability in one's career is increasingly outdated. Millennial workers must become comfortable with the idea of **reinventing themselves** periodically, whether by learning new technical skills or shifting to entirely different fields.

- **Invest in self-directed learning**: Platforms like **LinkedIn Learning**, **Coursera**, and **Skillshare** offer courses on everything from AI basics to advanced data science. Millennials can take advantage of these tools to upskill, reskill, and explore new areas of interest.

A **growth mindset** will allow you to see challenges as opportunities to expand your capabilities, both in your career and personal life. In an AI-driven world, where the future of work is constantly evolving, adaptability is the key to thriving.

Building Technical Literacy: From Basic Understanding to Mastery

While not everyone needs to become a **data scientist** or **AI engineer**, understanding the basics of AI is crucial for navigating the future job market. Millennials don't need to be intimidated by the complexity of AI but should aim to **build a foundation of technical literacy** that allows them to understand and work with AI tools effectively.

Understanding AI Fundamentals

AI is no longer a niche topic reserved for computer scientists. It is affecting nearly every sector—**finance, healthcare, education, marketing**, and even **the arts**. Here's how Millennials can start building a technical understanding:

- **Learn the basics of AI**: Free and accessible online courses like those on **edX** or **Udacity** can help you grasp foundational AI concepts. Understanding terms like **machine learning, neural networks**, and **data processing** will allow you to navigate the conversations and decisions that shape AI's role in your life.

- **Understand AI tools for non-tech professionals**: Many industries are integrating AI tools that are designed to be accessible to non-technical professionals. For example, **AI for marketing** (tools like **HubSpot** and **Hootsuite**) or **AI for content creation** (tools like **Copy.ai** and **Grammarly**) are already available to help you get ahead in your career without needing to be a technical expert.

- **Focus on human-AI collaboration**: Millennials should focus on how AI can augment their work rather than replace it. Building AI literacy will allow you to use AI to **enhance creativity, increase productivity**, and **solve problems**. The future of work is not about competing with machines but working alongside them.

In the workplace, technical literacy will allow you to remain **relevant**, make **data-driven decisions**, and **adapt** to new challenges. The more you understand how AI works, the better positioned you will be to collaborate with AI and make strategic decisions that benefit your career.

Cultivating Emotional Intelligence: AI Can't Replace Human Connection

As automation takes over routine tasks, one thing that machines will never replicate is the **human touch**. That's where emotional intelligence (EQ) comes in. Millennials, who are already known for their emphasis on **well-being, empathy**, and **relationship-building**, will thrive in an AI-driven world by cultivating their **emotional intelligence**.

AI can handle tasks that are repetitive, data-driven, or even creatively assisted, but **empathy, intuition**, and **human connection** are still deeply rooted in human experience. Millennials who invest in building their emotional intelligence will continue to have an edge in the workplace and personal relationships.

Why Emotional Intelligence is Essential in an AI World

- **Interpersonal skills**: Emotional intelligence allows you to better navigate complex social dynamics, resolve conflicts, and work in collaborative teams—skills that AI can't replicate. These "soft skills" will become even more valuable as automation takes over repetitive tasks.

- **Leadership and management**: AI can analyze data, but it can't inspire a team, create a vision, or provide meaningful mentorship. Leadership will be about **empathy, adaptability**, and **strategic vision**, qualities that are best nurtured through human experience.

- **Customer service and client relationships**: While chatbots and automated systems can handle many basic customer service queries, human connection will remain paramount for building long-term relationships with clients, customers, and colleagues.

Millennials who can blend technical proficiency with high emotional intelligence will be in high demand as leaders, collaborators, and relationship-builders.

Exploring New Career Paths and Entrepreneurial Opportunities

The AI revolution is not just about reshaping traditional job roles—it's also creating new **career paths** and **entrepreneurial opportunities**. For Millennials who are open to embracing change, this is a chance to **innovate** and **build** something entirely new.

New Career Pathways

As AI continues to evolve, entire industries will emerge that didn't exist just a few years ago. Some career paths that will be essential in an AI-driven world include:

- **AI Training and Oversight**: While AI systems can learn from data, they still require human oversight to ensure they function ethically and accurately. There will be a growing need for **AI ethicists**, **bias auditors**, and **AI trainers** who can teach AI systems to be effective and fair.

- **AI Human Collaboration Specialist**: As AI systems become more embedded into business operations, the demand for professionals who can facilitate **human-AI collaboration** will rise. These individuals will need to bridge the gap between machine intelligence and human creativity, optimizing workflows and ensuring that teams use AI to its fullest potential.

- **Data Privacy and Security Experts**: With AI's reliance on vast amounts of data, protecting that data will become even more critical. Careers focused on **data security**, **privacy**, and **cybersecurity** will continue to expand.

- **AI Health & Wellness Advisors**: As AI begins to impact healthcare, wellness, and personal well-being, there will be a need for **health professionals** who can integrate AI insights with **human-centered care**.

Entrepreneurship in an AI World

AI also offers unprecedented opportunities for Millennials who are entrepreneurial at heart. **AI as a service**, **automated products**, and **data-driven startups** are opening new doors for innovative ventures. Some potential opportunities include:

- **AI-Enhanced Startups**: If you have an entrepreneurial spirit, consider launching a startup that leverages AI to solve existing problems or improve an industry. Whether it's AI for health, education, or entertainment, innovation is the key to staying ahead.

- **Automation of Business Models**: Many small business owners are using AI-powered tools to streamline processes, handle customer service, and manage operations. This could lead to new **business models** where AI helps entrepreneurs scale faster, reach global markets, and reduce operational costs.

- **Creative Ventures**: AI is already being used in creative fields to generate art, music, and content. Entrepreneurs in the creative space can use AI to experiment with new forms of artistic expression, blending human creativity with machine intelligence to create novel experiences.

Future-Proofing Yourself in the AI Era

AI is transforming society in ways we can't fully predict, but one thing is clear: the most successful individuals will be those who **adapt**, **learn continuously**, and **embrace change**. Millennials, with their ability to think critically, challenge the status quo, and integrate new technologies, are uniquely positioned to lead in this new era.

To thrive in an AI-driven world, you need to focus on building a **growth mindset**, mastering technical literacy, cultivating emotional intelligence, and being open to new career opportunities and entrepreneurial ventures. By doing so, you will not just survive in the age of AI—you'll thrive, leading the charge toward a future where humans and machines work together to achieve remarkable things.

Chapter 10: Beyond the Job: Building a Fulfilling Life in the AI Era

AI is reshaping not just the workplace but every aspect of our lives. As we look to the future, it's important to think about how we can lead fulfilling, meaningful lives in this new world. This chapter discusses strategies for staying connected to your passions, hobbies, and relationships as you navigate the AI revolution.

The Moral Landscape of AI

As AI continues to evolve at breakneck speed, it brings with it a host of ethical challenges that society—especially Millennials—will need to navigate. Unlike previous technological revolutions, AI is not just a tool; it is rapidly becoming a **decision-maker**, influencing everything from hiring practices to healthcare outcomes and even **criminal justice**. The decisions made by AI systems, often driven by vast datasets, are shaping our futures in ways that are both exciting and, at times, deeply unsettling.

The increasing power of AI prompts fundamental questions about **who controls the technology, how it is used**, and **whether it aligns with values that benefit all of humanity**. As we move deeper into the AI era, the ethical implications of these systems will become more pressing. For Millennials, who are not only inheriting this world but are also instrumental in shaping it, engaging with these ethical questions is not just important—it's **imperative**.

In this chapter, we will explore how Millennials can engage with AI's ethical challenges, focusing on key issues like **bias**, **privacy**, **accountability**, **transparency**, and **social justice**. We'll also discuss how Millennials can act as ethical stewards, ensuring that AI is developed and deployed in ways that promote a more equitable, humane, and just society.

The Dangers of Bias in AI

AI systems, while incredibly powerful, are only as unbiased as the data they are trained on. Unfortunately, many datasets contain **biases**—reflecting societal prejudices related to race, gender, class, and more. These biases can seep into the algorithms that power AI, leading to **discriminatory outcomes** in critical areas like hiring, criminal justice, healthcare, and lending.

Examples of Bias in AI

- **Hiring Algorithms**: AI systems used to screen job applicants often reflect the biases of their creators. If a system is trained on data from industries where men are overrepresented in leadership roles, the AI may prioritize male candidates, perpetuating gender inequality in the workplace.

- **Criminal Justice**: AI systems used in predictive policing or sentencing risk assessments can amplify existing biases in the criminal justice system. For instance, if an algorithm is trained on historical arrest data, it may disproportionately target minority communities, perpetuating cycles of racial discrimination.

- **Healthcare**: AI in healthcare can lead to poor outcomes if it is trained on data that underrepresents certain populations. For example, if an algorithm used to recommend treatments for heart disease is trained on predominantly white male data, it may fail to accurately diagnose or treat women or people of color.

The Role of Millennials in Combating Bias

Millennials are uniquely positioned to address these biases because they understand the importance of **inclusivity** and **representation**. To combat bias in AI, Millennials can advocate for:

- **Diverse data sets**: Encourage the use of **representative data** in training AI algorithms, ensuring that they reflect the diversity of real-world populations.

- **Bias audits and accountability**: Support efforts to regularly audit AI systems for bias, and advocate for accountability measures when biases are detected.

- **Ethical AI design**: Promote the creation of **diverse teams** in AI development, ensuring that different perspectives are considered in the design and deployment of AI technologies.

As AI becomes increasingly integrated into everyday life, addressing bias in AI will be a crucial step in building a **fairer** and **more just society**.

Privacy and Data Protection: Safeguarding Our Digital Identities

In the age of AI, **data** is often referred to as the new oil, powering everything from targeted advertisements to advanced machine learning systems. But with this vast accumulation of data comes a significant ethical dilemma: how do we protect individual privacy in a world where our personal information is constantly being collected, analyzed, and monetized?

The Privacy Crisis

AI systems rely on access to massive amounts of data, much of which is deeply personal. **Social media platforms**, **search engines**, **financial institutions**, and even **smart devices** gather information about our habits, preferences, and daily activities. This data is used to create predictive models, recommend products, and make decisions on our behalf. However, the more data that's collected, the more vulnerable individuals become to breaches of privacy and **identity theft**.

For example, AI-driven facial recognition systems have raised significant concerns about **surveillance** and **anonymity**. While these technologies can be useful for security purposes, they also pose risks to personal privacy, especially when used without consent or transparency.

The Ethical Dilemma

- **Informed consent**: How much should companies disclose about how they are using your data? Millennials should demand greater **transparency** from companies about data collection practices and support the implementation of **clear consent** frameworks that allow users to understand and control how their data is being used.

- **Data ownership**: Who owns the data that is generated about us? Should it belong to the individual, the corporation, or some shared entity? The debate over data ownership will likely be one of the most important ethical discussions of the AI era.
- **Surveillance**: The rise of AI-powered surveillance technologies poses significant ethical questions. While these tools can increase safety and security, they can also infringe on personal freedoms and rights. Millennials can advocate for stronger regulations to protect privacy and prevent mass surveillance.

Millennials' Role in Defending Privacy

Millennials can take an active role in **advocating for privacy** by supporting **privacy-first technologies** and **policies**. Efforts like the **General Data Protection Regulation (GDPR)** in Europe have set a global standard for data privacy, and Millennials can push for similar protections in other regions. Moreover, they can use **privacy-conscious tools**—from encrypted messaging services to **VPNs**—to protect their own personal data.

Ultimately, the fight for privacy in an AI-driven world will require a balance between innovation and individual rights. Millennials can lead the charge in making privacy protection an **ethical imperative**.

Transparency and Accountability: The Need for Clear AI Governance

AI systems can be complex and opaque, often described as "black boxes" because even their creators may not fully understand how the algorithm makes decisions. This lack of transparency raises critical ethical questions about **accountability** and **responsibility** when AI systems make mistakes or harm individuals.

The Problem of the Black Box

- **Opaque decision-making**: AI systems often make decisions based on data patterns that are not easily interpretable by humans. In high-stakes areas like healthcare or criminal justice, these "black-box" algorithms can make life-altering decisions without sufficient human oversight, leading to potential harm.

- **Algorithmic accountability**: When an AI system makes an erroneous or biased decision, who is responsible? Is it the developer who created the algorithm, the company that deployed it, or the machine itself? AI accountability remains a significant ethical challenge, particularly when algorithms lead to negative outcomes.

Millennials and the Call for Transparency

Millennials, particularly those in tech or policy-making roles, can drive the demand for **transparent AI** by pushing for clearer **explanations** of how AI systems make decisions. Some practical steps include:

- **Open-source AI**: Advocate for the development of open-source AI projects that make algorithms and data accessible to the public, encouraging transparency and accountability.

- **Explainability**: Support the development of AI systems that prioritize **explainability**—AI that can clearly justify its decisions in understandable terms for non-experts.

Millennials can also support **public oversight** of AI systems, pushing for the creation of **regulatory bodies** that monitor AI development and ensure it is used responsibly. By promoting AI that is explainable, accountable, and governed by ethical standards, Millennials can ensure that AI remains a tool for **positive social change**.

AI and Social Justice: Ensuring AI Benefits All of Humanity

AI has the potential to reshape not only individual lives but entire societies. However, as with any technological advancement, there's a risk that AI could disproportionately benefit the already privileged and exacerbate existing inequalities. To ensure that AI contributes to a fairer, more just world, it is crucial to address issues of **equity**, **accessibility**, and **inclusivity**.

The Risk of Widening Inequality

- **Access to AI technology**: Not everyone has equal access to the tools and resources that make AI beneficial. While some industries and individuals are leveraging AI to drive innovation and profit, many communities, particularly low-income and marginalized groups, are left behind in this digital divide.

- **Bias in AI applications**: As mentioned earlier, biased algorithms can reinforce existing social inequalities. For instance, AI in hiring or criminal justice can disproportionately impact people of color or women, further entrenching systemic inequities.

Millennials and Social Justice in AI

Millennials can ensure that AI benefits **all** of humanity, not just the privileged few, by:

- **Advocating for inclusive AI development**: Encourage the creation of AI systems that serve a wide range of communities, including marginalized and underserved populations.

- **Promoting access to AI education**: Support initiatives that provide access to AI education and training for underserved communities, empowering more people to participate in and benefit from the AI revolution.

- **Supporting AI for social good**: Invest in and advocate for AI projects that address pressing global challenges, such as **climate change**, **poverty**, and **public health**.

Millennials have an opportunity to ensure that AI is used as a **force for good**, working toward a more **equitable**, **inclusive**, and **just society**. By advocating for social justice in AI development and ensuring that everyone benefits from these technologies, Millennials can help guide the ethical use of AI in the years ahead.

Leading the Charge for Ethical AI

The future of AI is not predetermined; it will be shaped by the decisions we make today. Millennials have a unique opportunity to engage with the ethical challenges of AI, ensuring that its development aligns with values like **equity**, **inclusivity**, **transparency**, and **social justice**. By advocating for **fairness**,

privacy, and **accountability**, Millennials can ensure that AI evolves into a force that **empowers** humanity rather than undermines it.

As we look ahead to a world where AI is deeply integrated into every aspect of our lives, the ethical choices we make now will determine whether AI creates a **better world** or a **worse one**. By leading with responsibility, care, and empathy, Millennials can shape an AI-powered future that is not only innovative and efficient but also **just**, **humane**, and **equitable**.

Conclusion: Moving Forward with Confidence in the Age of AI

The rise of AI isn't something to fear — it's something to embrace. With the right mindset, tools, and strategies, you can thrive in this new world. It's about leveraging your unique strengths, learning new skills, and adapting to change. The future isn't set in stone, and with the right approach, you can not only keep up with AI but use it to your advantage.

Welcome to the future. Let's make sure we don't just survive — we thrive.

As we close this book, it's essential to reflect on the practical steps Millennials can take to not just **keep up** with the changes AI is bringing to the world, but to **thrive** within it. AI is here to stay, and it is shaping every industry, every job, and even our daily lives in profound ways. The key to ensuring that Millennials are not left behind in this rapidly changing landscape is to take **purposeful**

action today to build the skills, mindset, and ethical foundation that will propel us into the future.

In this final section, we will distill the insights from throughout the book into actionable steps Millennials can take to future-proof their careers, contribute to a more equitable society, and harness the potential of AI in ways that benefit **themselves**, **their communities**, and **the world**.

1. Invest in Lifelong Learning: The Bedrock of Adaptability

AI is transforming industries so quickly that the skills in demand today may be outdated tomorrow. The first and most crucial step to ensuring you don't get left behind is committing to **lifelong learning**. This is not just about keeping your knowledge current, but actively seeking new areas of knowledge that align with your passions, your career goals, and the future of work.

Practical Steps:

- **Enroll in Online Courses**: Platforms like **Coursera, Udemy, edX**, and **LinkedIn Learning** provide access to affordable courses on everything from AI fundamentals to specialized skills like machine learning, data science, and ethical AI. Take advantage of free trials and certifications to build a portfolio of relevant skills.

- **Learn the Basics of AI and Data Literacy**: Even if you don't plan on becoming an AI developer, understanding how AI works is critical. Familiarize yourself with key concepts like **machine learning, neural networks**, and **natural language processing**. Understanding the *language* of AI will help you stay competitive in many industries.

- **Master Problem-Solving and Critical Thinking**: AI might automate tasks, but **creative problem-solving, empathy**, and **critical thinking** are inherently human skills that will remain indispensable. Invest in developing these cognitive skills through continuous education and real-world application.

By proactively learning, you'll not only stay relevant in your field but position yourself as a forward-thinking leader ready to adapt to the evolving demands of AI-powered industries.

2. Cultivate Emotional Intelligence and Soft Skills

AI can do many things—analyze data, automate processes, and even create art. However, it can never replace **human connection, empathy**, and **emotional intelligence**. These are the soft skills that Millennials already excel at and that will become even more valuable as AI takes over routine tasks.

Practical Steps:

- **Develop Communication Skills**: Whether it's through public speaking, writing, or interpersonal communication, honing your ability to communicate effectively will always set you apart. AI can process information, but it can't tell a story or connect emotionally in the way humans can.

- **Focus on Emotional Intelligence (EQ)**: Understand how to manage your own emotions and respond to others in ways that build trust, collaboration, and empathy. Emotional intelligence will help you succeed in leadership roles, customer service, teamwork, and client relationships.

- **Seek Mentorship**: Build relationships with people who inspire you. Seek out mentors who can help you navigate both the technical and emotional challenges of the AI-driven future.

In an AI-driven world, the human touch will always be irreplaceable. By cultivating emotional intelligence and soft skills, Millennials can leverage their natural strengths to maintain their value in an increasingly automated world.

3. Build a Digital Presence and Personal Brand

AI may be reshaping industries, but it's also opening up new ways to **connect** and **build a personal brand**. Millennials, who are already digitally savvy, are in a unique position to use AI tools to showcase their skills, expertise, and values. Whether you're a **freelancer, entrepreneur**, or professional, building an authentic digital presence can increase your visibility and open up career opportunities.

Practical Steps:

- **Create an Online Portfolio**: Build a website or personal blog that highlights your work, skills, and projects. Use platforms like **LinkedIn, Behance**, or **GitHub** to showcase your expertise in a professional manner.
- **Engage on Social Media**: Use platforms like **Twitter, Instagram**, and **Medium** to engage with industry leaders, share your insights, and stay informed on AI and related topics. Being part of the conversation will help you stay connected and visible.

- **Leverage AI Tools**: Utilize AI-powered tools like **Canva** for design, **Grammarly** for writing, or **Hootsuite** for social media management. These tools can save time and enhance your work, allowing you to focus on creative and strategic tasks that machines can't replicate.

Your personal brand is your reputation in the digital world, and AI can help you amplify that brand. Millennials can use technology to their advantage by consistently showcasing their skills, creativity, and unique perspective online.

4. Embrace New Career Opportunities and Entrepreneurial Ventures

AI is transforming traditional industries and creating entirely new career pathways. While many jobs will be automated, new roles are being created in fields such as **AI ethics, data privacy, AI implementation**, and **human-AI collaboration**. Additionally, Millennials have a strong entrepreneurial spirit that positions them well to take advantage of new business opportunities powered by AI.

Practical Steps:

- **Explore Emerging Fields**: Research the most promising careers in AI and technology. Some examples include **AI ethics specialists, data privacy officers, AI business consultants, AI trainers**, and **human-machine interface designers**.

- **Launch an AI-Driven Startup**: If you have an entrepreneurial mindset, AI offers a world of opportunities. Think about how you can create solutions that use AI to address unmet needs, whether it's in **healthcare, education, sustainability**, or **entertainment**.

- **Develop a Side Hustle**: Leverage AI-powered tools and platforms to develop a side business that's based on your passions. From **content creation** to **online education** to **AI-enhanced consulting**, there's a wealth of opportunities to build a sustainable income stream.

AI will undoubtedly disrupt traditional job markets, but with the right mindset and entrepreneurial approach, Millennials can harness the technology to build **innovative careers** and businesses.

5. Advocate for Ethical AI Development and Use

Millennials are deeply invested in creating a more **equitable**, **inclusive**, and **sustainable** world. As AI continues to advance, the need for ethical guidelines and governance will be more important than ever. Millennials must not only **learn** about AI but also actively engage in shaping its future to ensure that it reflects **our shared values** of fairness, justice, and compassion.

Practical Steps:

- **Stay Informed on AI Ethics**: Follow thought leaders, read research, and attend conferences or webinars on AI ethics, transparency, and bias. Stay informed about the latest issues, and advocate for policies that ensure AI is developed and used responsibly.

- **Push for Ethical AI in the Workplace**: If you're in a tech or business role, be a champion for **ethical AI practices**. Advocate for **inclusive datasets**, **bias audits**, and **clear accountability** when developing or using AI systems.

- **Participate in AI Governance**: Get involved in discussions about **AI regulation**, **data privacy**, and **social justice** by joining professional organizations, attending workshops, and advocating for policies that prioritize ethical standards in AI development.

As the next generation of workers, leaders, and citizens, Millennials have the power to shape the direction of AI. By pushing for ethical practices and fair governance, we can ensure that AI serves the collective good rather than reinforcing existing inequalities.

6. Foster Collaboration Between Humans and AI

Rather than viewing AI as a competitor, Millennials should embrace the opportunities for **collaboration** between humans and machines. AI can enhance human creativity, automate mundane tasks, and solve complex problems. The future will be shaped by **human-AI partnerships** that combine the best of both worlds: human ingenuity and machine efficiency.

Practical Steps:

- **Learn to Work with AI Tools**: AI is increasingly integrated into everyday tools in business, marketing, and the arts. Learn how to use **AI-powered productivity tools** to enhance your workflow, such as **GPT-driven writing assistants** or **AI-based data analysis platforms**.

- **Focus on Creativity and Innovation**: While AI can automate repetitive tasks, it excels when paired with **human creativity**. Use AI to augment your artistic, strategic, or entrepreneurial work. Let AI handle the technical details, so you can focus on **big-picture thinking** and **innovative problem-solving**.

- **Collaborate Across Disciplines**: The future of work will be **interdisciplinary**. If you have a background in **the humanities**, consider how your insights into ethics, communication, and culture can enrich AI development. If you're a **tech expert**, collaborate with others to bring AI to life in socially meaningful ways.

By approaching AI as a partner, Millennials can harness its potential to create a better world, drive innovation, and make a lasting impact.

Final Thoughts: Embrace the Future with Purpose

The rise of AI offers both incredible opportunities and significant challenges. For Millennials, the key to not getting left behind in this new world is to **take action now**. By focusing on continuous learning, developing emotional intelligence, embracing new career paths, and advocating for ethical AI, Millennials can shape the future rather than be shaped by it.

The journey ahead may be uncertain, but one thing is clear: **the future belongs to those who adapt**, to those who understand how to work alongside AI, and to those who are willing to ensure that AI benefits **all** of humanity.

The choice is yours—**lead the charge** or be left behind. Choose to thrive. Choose to innovate. Choose to create a future where humans and machines work together to build a better, more equitable world.

Final Thought:

The key takeaway? AI isn't here to replace you — it's here to work with you. Embrace the change. Learn constantly. Adapt. And above all, continue to use the incredible human qualities that make you unique.

It's your time to shine.